LEAN ON ME

A MESSAGE OF HOPE TO HUMANITY

MILLICENT ADANNE CHUKWU

authorHOUSE®

AuthorHouse™ UK
1663 Liberty Drive
Bloomington, IN 47403 USA
www.authorhouse.co.uk
Phone: 0800 047 8203 (Domestic TFN)
        +44 1908 723714 (International)

Published by AuthorHouse   05/06/2020

ISBN: 978-1-7283-5207-7 (sc)
ISBN: 978-1-7283-5206-0 (e)

CONTENTS

FOREWORD

I give glory to Jesus and honour to the Blessed Virgin Mary; having been asked by the National Youth Service Corps (NYSC) member, "Corper" Millicent Chukwu to write a forward to her maiden book *"Lean on me"*. For me, the theme of this book is colossally topical.

At a time when the social, political, economic and even spiritual atmosphere is so discouraging in our country, Nigeria; when our leaders have failed us, secular and spiritual; when friends have disappointed us, etc., which hitherto hassled many to now depend on their strength, money, ingenuity; when materialism is now the order of the day, the book *"Lean on Me"* shows the way out. It is a clarion call on all and sundry to depend solely on Christ, who tells us:

> *"Come to me all who labour and overburdened and I will give you rest"* (Matthew 11:28).

The book is a sincere effort by this young author to expose the willingness in Christ to assist believers who will *lean on him*. This book will certainly touch many lives. I am convinced that this book is borne out of the wealth of experience of the author as a believer in Christ herself.

I strongly recommend this book wholeheartedly to all, Christians and non-Christians alike, as I think she deserves our gratitude and encouragement.

Rev. Fr. Cyprian Onah Oko
St. Charles Catholic Church,
Obudu Parish, Cross River State
July, 2005.

ACKNOWLEDGEMENT

I wish to express my profound gratitude to God Almighty for his love and faithfulness throughout my service year. To God be all the glory.

I owe a lot of thanks to my beloved and wonderful Mum, Mrs. Eunice Oby Chukwu, for her untiring effort to give me the best in life. Remain blessed Mum. My late Dad, Mr. Benneth Obioma Chukwu, can never be forgotten. May your gentle soul continue to rest in perfect peace Dad; Amen.

In a special way, I wish to sincerely thank Rev. Fr. Emmanuel Odey (Parish Priest, St. Charles Catholic Church, Obudu) and his Assistant, Rev Fr. Cyprian Onah Oko, for creating time to go through my work and for their fatherly advice, care and support during my service year in Obudu/Obanliku L.G.A, Cross-River State.

Thankfully, I acknowledge the encouragement and support from Engr. E. U. Onochie and family, who laid the solid foundation upon which my academic life is built. Remain blessed Daddy Onochie.

My special thanks go to Mr. & Mrs. (Lolo) White Iheagwam, Mr. & Mrs. Nwafor Isioha for their wonderful support in making this publication a reality. I wish to sincerely thank Dr. & Mrs. Mark Omu, Mr. & Mrs. Sunny Okoro, Elder & Mrs. Agbarevo, Mr. & Mrs. S.E. Okoye, Aunt Ugoeze (Miracle) for their love, care and support during my service year.

I also recognize and appreciate the support and prayers of Rev. Fr. (Dr.) Augustus Essien, Rev. Fr. Innocent Abonyi, Rev. Fr. Zachariah Samjumi, Rev. Fr. Francis Nass, Rev. Fr. Attah Barkindo, Rev. Fr. Martins Hayatu, all the members of Peace

Prayer Group Yola, of the Catholic Charismatic Renewal of Nigeria, Rev. Fr. Moses Taparki, Rev Sr. Mary Tuku (HHCJ), Rev Sr, Rose Abang, Mr & Mrs C.Y Chukwudum, Bro. Clems Okafor & family, Bro. Livinus & Okechukwu Tagbo, Lady Nkechi Umeohana, Mrs. Chinelo Ukadike, Mrs. Christy Kenkwo, Bro Innocent Igwilo, Bro. Emmanuel Chukwu, and my beloved Michael's Dad.

My special thanks go to my wonderful sisters, Nkechi, Chinenye, Chinonyelum, Oluchi, my daughter Miracle (Mimi), my darling brother Ekene, my nephew Little Chinonso, my cousins: Josephat (Emmy) and Chinedum, for their love and support while in school and throughout my service year.

Finally, I wish to thank Mr. Femi Idowu, Dr. S.A. Okparaocha, fellow corps members and my friends especially Franca Anakwuba, Frank Igwe, Uche Okoye, Ojinika Amadi, Chika Nganyadi, Peter Otese, Chuka Chiezie, Nnamdi Onah, Prisliv Obiegbu, Dr Umeh, Austine Dickson, Pharm: Philip, Chris, Chamberlin Onuoha and Barr. Theo Okpara (CLO). Thanks to my students, especially Elijah Uchua, Moses, Simon and Angel. Thanks to Celestine Abaka Uyimke who typed my manuscript and to all who contributed in any way towards making this publication a very successful one.

May God bless you all abundantly in Jesus name, Amen.

DEDICATION

This book *"Lean on Me"* is dedicated to **The Holy Trinity:** my source of strength, hope, knowledge, and inspiration; who has lifted me from the deepest part of the pit to palaces and has made my wonderful dreams come true.

INTRODUCTION

The world is really dynamic in nature as the situation of things vary with different people and at different times. Sometimes, the going is smooth and steady. Other times, it is tough and thorny; yet other times, it is a mixed grill of the good and the bad. This book however aims at giving hope to the hopeless, especially when the going is tough. Many people have misplaced their priorities in life and have placed their ray of hope on so many things, which at last failed them woefully. Many have vowed never to trust other people due to the many disappointments they have faced in life. The worst is that some of these people even doubt God's ability because of the betrayals they have encountered in life. The book aims at letting people realise that it is only God that cannot fail if leaned on sincerely, comfortably and whole-heartedly. Christ himself threw an open invitation to those who labour and are over-burdened, that he will give them rest and lighten their loads as recorded in the Gospel of Matthew 11:28, EXB.

In John 15:5, GNT, Jesus says: *"I am the vine and you are the branches. Those who remain in me, and I in them will bear much fruit; for you can do nothing without me"*. Also, verse 7 of that same chapter says: **If you remain in me,** in other words, **if you lean on me, and my** *words remain in you, then you will ask for anything you wish, and you shall have it"*. Besides, in John 8:12, CSB, Jesus says: *"I am the light of the world, anyone who follows me will never walk in darkness, but will have the light of life"*. The above passages show that Christ is appealing to each and every one of us to lean on him and live.

The book goes further to analyse some instances of those

who Leaned on transitory things rather than the Most High God and were greatly disappointed.

Notwithstanding, there is a divine link, between "leaning on the Most High God" and "Victory". This was discovered from the survey of those who sincerely leaned on God and were favoured. One of the examples given is a true-life story of a man whose heart was damaged due to certain diseases and the best doctors predicted when he would die but due to his trust in the Lord, God made a new heart develop and replaced the bad one miraculously; afterwards the man lived beyond the doctor's predicted time because the Doctor of all doctors handled his case. Surely, there is a divine correlation between "leaning on the Most High God" and "victory" because all that leaned on God were victorious at last despite the troubles encountered.

Christ remains the Hope of the hopeless and has promised never to forget you, no matter the troubles you have faced in life or you are still facing presently. He said in 1 Cor 10:13, GNT that *"Every temptation that you have experienced is the kind that normally comes to people. But God keeps his promise, and he will not allow you to be tempted beyond your power to remain firm; at the time you're being put to the test, he will give you the strength to endure it and so provide you with a way out"*. Jesus has never failed anyone who put his/her trust in him and you will not be an exception. He will definitely make uncountable number of ways where there is absolutely none for you if you lean on him sincerely. There is need to do away with fear at all times because fear is often associated with doubt, anxiety and failure rather we ought to have absolute faith in God Almighty who can make the impossible very possible.

Finally, this book aims at resuscitating *"dead lives"*; it is an expose to the dynamics of life as it presents us with the clues that would help us understand the realities of life, above which is God who remains infallible. It also reminds us of God's infinite love, his faithfulness, promises and assurances. Most importantly, it reveals the great power in the **WORD,** which every one of us should ***lean on*** because the Word of God is God himself (John 1:1).

Thank you, Jesus!

CHAPTER 1

THE SUPREMACY OF GOD

O ur God is indeed supreme in all sense of the word. Just imagine the Creator of the whole universe, all things being created out of nothing but through his words. Many, I guess, would have imagined the origin of God. I had imagined that several times as a growing child without any satisfactory answers until I began to explore the scriptures which has the answers to everything. The gospel of John 1:1 – 5, GNT clarified such ambiguous thoughts in us thus: *"In the beginning the Word already existed; the Word was with God, and the Word was God. From the very beginning the Word was with God. Through him God made all things; not one thing in all creation was made without him. The Word was the source of life, and this life brought life to humanity. The light shines in the darkness, and the darkness has never put it out".* We can infer from the passage that God is the beginning himself.

In Genesis 1:1-31; and 2:1-4, GNT, the whole world and all in it were created by God as outlined in the passages, thus:

> *"In the beginning, when God created the universe, the earth was formless and desolate. The raging ocean that covered everything was engulfed in total darkness, and*

the spirit of God was moving over the water. Then God commanded, "Let there be light" and light appeared. God was pleased with what he saw. Then he separated the light from the darkness and he named the light "Day" and the darkness "Night". This happened on the first day of creation. On the second day of creation, God commanded that there be a dome to divide the water and to keep it in two separate places, it was done and he named the dome "sky".

The third day, the Lord created the earth, the sea, and further commanded that all kinds of fruits be produced by commanding lights to appear in the sky in order to separate day from night and to show the time when days, years and religious festivals begin. The Lord also created the sun to rule over the day and the moon to rule over the night. He also made the stars. All these took place on the fourth day.

On the fifth day however, the Lord created all kinds of creatures that live inside the water and all kinds of birds. He blessed them all and told the creatures that live in water to reproduce and fill the sea, and he told the birds to increase in number.

However, on the sixth day, God commanded the earth to produce all kinds of animal life; domestic and wild, large and small. He further created human beings in his image and likeness, to have power over the fish, the birds, and all animals, domestic and wild, large and small. He created them male and female, blessed them and said, "Have many children, so that your descendants will live all over the earth and bring it under their control. I am putting you in charge of the fish, the birds, and all the wild animals. I have provided all kinds of grain and all kinds of fruit for you to eat; but for all the wild animals and for all the birds I have provided grass and leafy plants for food." All these happened as the Lord commanded.

When the Lord completed the creation of the universe, he rested on the seventh day and set it apart as a special day.

Is that not wonderful of God? I would like you to just ponder a while the passage you've just gone through about our dear Lord and the creation of the whole universe. Can you measure or assume the length and breadth of the whole world? The measurement of the world given is even referred to as that of the observable universe. This shows that there is also the unobservable part of the universe, known best by the creator himself. Looking at the world literally, what kind of pillar(s) can you imagine that is used to hold the universe in order to prevent it from collapsing? Gravity, you may say but then have you thought of the origin of that gravity itself. Have you ever imagined how God created human beings uniquely out of all other kinds of animals in the whole world? Think also about the differences in human beings, even people of the same parents have their own individual and unique differences. Identical twins also have their individual differences as well. Think of how God attends to the uncountable number of millions of people at the same time in prayers. God is indeed "too much". I am yet to get a satisfactory adjective with which to quality God because his greatness is beyond human understanding, highly inestimable.

God is omnipotent. He indeed has the total power and ability to do everything. In Jeremiah 32:17, GNT, Jeremiah prayed, ***"Sovereign Lord, you made the earth and the sky by your great power and might; nothing is too difficult for you".***

Absolutely, there is nothing that the Lord cannot do. It is you and I that limit God's ability. We have no cause to be afraid of anything/anybody order than the Most High and All Powerful God who can do many things out of nothing. No one can neither close any door in your life, which God has opened, nor open any closed door by God because He has the final say. He is our Last Resort.

God also proved his supreme nature in Exodus 4:1 – 31 – *"Crossing the Red Sea".* The Lord delivered the Israelites from the hands of the Egyptians by making way for the Israelites through the Red Sea while the Egyptians were drowned in the cause of crossing. They laid dead on the seashore. When the Israelites saw the great power with which the Lord had defeated the Egyptians, they stood in awe of the Lord and had faith in God and in his servant Moses.

God is also Omnipresent and Omniscient. In other words, he is everywhere and knows everything. There is absolutely nothing that can happen without the knowledge of God. Remember Adam and Eve in the Garden of Eden as recorded in Genesis 3: 1 – 21. When they ate the fruit, which God forbade them from eating, they realised that they were naked and sewed fig leaves to cover themselves. That evening, they heard the Lord God walking in the garden, and they hid from him among the trees. The All-Knowing God discovered them from their hiding place. The man blamed the woman while the woman shifted her own blame on the serpent. The punishment, which God pronounced on each of them, holds till today as we can notice that the serpent feeds on dust and still drags its belly on the ground, and also remains one of man's greatest enemies. The women, of course, remained subject to their husbands, and the pain they go through during childbearing is unimaginable. Men, on the other hand, suffer a lot in order to make ends meet.

Glory to God, who has redeemed us by the precious Blood of Jesus Christ. God indeed has the total power as well as the final say in everything. He is indeed a perfect God that has never and can never change. From generation to generation, he remains the same. Whatever he says, he does, and none can challenge him. Isaiah 40:3, GNT says: *"Yes, grass withers and flowers fade but the Word of God endures forever".*

When Job challenged God due to his sufferings, the Lord called him to order by saying: *"Job, you challenged Almighty God; will you give up now or will you answer?"* Job said: *"I spoke foolishly, Lord, what can I answer? I will not try to say anything else. I have already said more than I should."* Then the Lord continued: "... **Look at the monster Behemoth; I created him and I created you. He eats grass like a cow but what strength there is in his body, and what power there is in his muscles! His tail stands up like a cedar, and the muscles in his legs are strong. The bones are as strong as bronze, and his legs are like iron bars. The most amazing of all my creatures! ONLY HIS CREATOR CAN DEFEAT HIM. (God is indeed supreme). Grass to feed him grows on the hills where wild beast play. He lies down under the thorn bushes, and hides among the reeds in the swamp. The thorn bushes and the willows by the stream give him shelter in their shade. He is not afraid of a rushing river; he is calm when the Jordan dashes in his face. Who can blind his eyes and capture him? Or who can catch his snout in a trap?"**

However, the Lord went further to tell Job about another fearless creature called Leviathan in Job 41:1 – 34; 42: 1, GNT, *that anyone who sees Leviathan loses courage and falls to the ground when he is aroused, he is fierce; no one would dear attack him and still be safe? No one can tear off his outer coat or pierce the armour he wears. No one can also make him open his jaws that are ringed with terrifying teeth. His back is made of rows of shields fastened together and hard as stone. Each one is joined so tight to the next that even a breath cannot come between. Light flashes when he sneezes and his eyes glow like the rising sun. Flames blaze from his mouth and streams of sparks fly out. Smoke comes out of his nose like smoke from weeds burning under a pot. His breath starts fires burning, flames leap out of his mouth. His stony heart is without fear, as unyielding and hard as a millstone. When he rises up, even the strongest are frightened; they are helpless with fear, there is no sword that can wound him, no spear or arrow or lance that can harm him. For him iron is as flimsy as straw, and bronze as soft as rotten wood. There is no arrow that can make him run; rocks thrown at him are like bits of straw. To him a club is a piece of straw, and he laughs when men throw spears. The scales on his belly are like jagged pieces of pottery; they tear up the muddy ground like a threshing-sledge. He churns up the sea like boiling water and makes it bubble like a pot of oil. He leaves a shining path behind him and turns the sea to white foam. There is nothing on earth to be compared with him; he is a creature that has no fear. He looks down on even the proudest animals. He is the king of all wild beasts.*

When the Lord finished telling Job about these creatures, then job exclaimed: ***"I know, Lord, that you are all-powerful; that you can do everything you want.... So, I am ashamed of all I have said and repent in dust and ashes"***

Oh! I will continue to exclaim that God is ***"too much"***. Only him has control over all his creatures and the entire universe. You can imagine how fierce the two aforementioned beasts are, with their terrifying characteristics and it is God alone who has the supreme power over them. There are different kinds of "beasts" in our lives which sometimes weigh us down as well as prove that there is no other way out. Reflect through your mind and imagine those *"beasts"* that have been making you have sleepless nights, causing you heart ache for a long time, the *"beast"* that has broken your marriage and has turned all your family members apart, the *"beast"* of failure, the *"beast"* of sickness. Is it the *"beast"* of late marriage? Is it the beast of childlessness? Is it the beast of poverty? Or the *"beast"* of sin generally? Whatever kind of *"beast"* in your life, just know that it is completely submissive to the creator of the world because God is supreme indeed over the whole universe. His yes remains yes, and his "no" remains no as well. No one can ever alter what God has instituted for you. God has the total power and the final say. In Isaiah 43:13, GNT God says: ***"I am God and always will be. No one can escape from my power; no one can change what I do".***

Job 9:4 GNT says: ***"God is so wise and powerful; no one can stand up against him".*** Verses 7, 8 and 10 say: ***"He can keep the sun from rising and the stars from shining at night. No one helped God spread out the heavens or trample the sea monster's back. We cannot understand the great things he does, and to his miracles, there is no end".*** Also, in Numbers 11:23, GNT, the Lord says: ***"Is there a limit to my power? You will soon see whether what I have said will happen or not!"*** In the presence of the Lord, mountains melt like wax and at the mention of the name of our Lord Jesus Christ, every knee must bow, and every tongue confesses that he is the Lord to the glory of God the Father. Just acknowledge the fact that none of the *"beasts"* in your life, irrespective of its magnitude, can withstand the presence of God due to his ability to do everything; then see it done.

However, there are so many things that portray the supreme nature of God on earth to the extent that I cannot give account of the uncountable number of them. Who am I in the first place and how deep or sharp is my little brain to understand fully the supremacy/personality of God? This is just the tip of an iceberg in order to help us realize that God is too great and no power can be compared with his. There is every need, therefore, to trust fully in God, follow his ways and allow him to take the lead in our lives; things would definitely change for the best.

CHAPTER 2

GOD'S FAITHFULNESS AND THE DYNAMIC WORLD

The world is really dynamic in nature as the situation of things varies at different times in different people, but God's faithfulness remains static. God does not change, and that is why he is often referred to as *"The Unchangeable Changer"* who is able to transform all things effortlessly. From generation to generation, the Lord remains the same. Two great philosophers – Cratylus and Heraclitus – propounded that change is inevitable and that everything is constantly on the move. In other words, the only thing that is constant in this world is *"change"*. It is a continuous process. This philosophy does not hold with God. He is an exception to that because, since the inception of the world, so many things have changed drastically with time, but God has never changed as well as his faithfulness to all his creatures.

However, in the time of old, people lived longer on earth. Typical examples can be found in the book of Genesis 5. It was recorded that Adam, the first man on earth, died at the age of

930. One of his sons, Seth, died at the age of 912. Another of his descendants, Enosh, lived 905 years on earth. Kenan died at the age of 910. Mahalal died at the age of 895. Jared, the father of Enoch, died at the age of 962. Enoch, the father of Methuselah, lived 365 years before disappearing because he spent his life in fellowship with God. Methuselah also had a son, Lamech, when he was 187 and then lived another 782 years. He had other children and died at the age of 969. He lived the longest time on earth.

In addition, Noah, the ark builder, lived 950 years on earth. As more years rolled by, the number of years people lived on earth continued to decline. In Genesis 23:1 and 25:7 – 8, the Bible recorded that Abraham, the father of all nations, and Sarah, the mother of all nations, lived 175 years on earth and 127 years respectively. This is just to mention but a few. In our present-day world, people rarely reach the age of 100 or above before transiting to the next world. Also, in the past, the death rate was very low even though medical facilities have improved now than in the past. It was always very difficult before someone dies, and when anyone dies, people feel the impact a lot. Presently, the reverse is always the case. Things have changed drastically to the extent that death impact is rarely felt and the death rate is also high now.

Furthermore, coming back home, i.e., analysing the changing situation in our own country, Nigeria, we can see that things have so much changed since Nigeria was amalgamated in 1914. Nigerian situation was never the same since then. Since 1960, about fifteen presidents have been on the presidential seat. The present president of the country will soon hand over to the next president. This change of leadership remains constant. In the whole world, we have different continents as well as various countries in each continent. All the leaders/rulers of these countries change with time as well. The systems of government also vary with time among different countries. The system of education also keeps changing from time to time in different parts of the world. In Nigeria, it has changed from different systems in the past to the present 6-3-3-4 system of education. So many activities, as well as some cultures, have changed from the old and primitive pattern to sophisticated/modern ways. The point I am trying to arrive at is the fact that the world and its activities keep revolving round and round day-in-day-out.

Notwithstanding, the Most-High God and his faithfulness to all his creatures remain static as aforementioned. So many kings and rulers in the world have been succeeded by others, and the kingship keeps rotating. Please have you ever heard that God can be or has ever been succeeded by any other king? Definitely not in this life and even in the life after! He remains the only King of the Universe and can never change even though things and activities are constantly on the move.

However, the static nature of God's faithfulness is incomparable. He is always faithful even when we are unfaithful to him; talk more of when we try to exhibit our own atom of faithfulness. He has promised to remain faithful to us until the end of time. The Lord assures us of his love and faithfulness at all times. In Isa 43:1 – 5, GNT, the Lord says: *"Israel (mention your name), the Lord who created you says, do not be afraid – I will save you. I have called you by name, you are mine. When you pass through deep waters, I will be with you; your troubles will not overwhelm you. When you pass through the fire, you will not be burnt; the hard trial that comes will not hurt you. For I am the Lord your God, the Holy God of Israel who saves you. I will give up Egypt to set you free; I will give up Sudan and Seba. I will give up whole nations to save your life BECAUSE YOU ARE PRECIOUS TO ME AND BECAUSE I LOVE*

YOU AND GIVE YOU HONOUR. Do not be afraid, I am with you". How do you feel on hearing these comforting words from our Lord? I guess you feel great; you are reassured of God's infinite love on his creatures, especially we, the human beings whom he created in his own image and likeness. Personally, I feel cool on realizing that God knows me by name; I feel completely secured. I believe you felt same as well because the Lord recognizes each and every one of us in this world, irrespective of our tribes, races, qualifications, position in the society; not even minding our physical structure, level of education, etc. He has declared that you are precious to him and that he loves you.

In Acts 10:34, GNT, Peter says: *"I now realize that it is true that God treats everyone on the same basis. Those who worship him and do what is right are acceptable to him, no matter what race they belong."* In-so-far-as we are in this world; one of the things that are inevitable is temptation. Sometimes, it comes in chains as though there would be no way out. Just always remember what God says in the above passages; that your trials and troubles will not overwhelm you and that he will give up everything in order to set you free, and crowned it all by telling you not to be afraid for he is with you. When God is with you, nothing can ever be against you. In Isaiah 43:13, CEV, God says: *"I am God for ever. Everything is under my power. No one can change my actions"*. In the actual sense of the word, no one at all can withstand God in any way his plans for you are perfect and wonderful as recorded in Jeremiah 29:11 – 14, GNT. *"I alone know the plans I have for you, plans to bring you prosperity and not disaster, plans to bring about the future you hope for. Then you will call to me you will come and pray to me and I will answer you. You will seek me and you will find me because you will seek me with all your heart. Yes, I say, you will find me and I will restore you to your land. I will gather you from every place to which I have scattered you and I will bring you back to the land from which I had sent you away into exile. I, the LORD, have spoken".*

Oh! Why worry about the changing situations in the world? Why are you so disturbed because you were living very comfortably before and now the comfort is gone? Are you worried because when your husband was alive, you had all you needed and when he died, the family members left you empty handed to suffer alone for your children? Are you worried because all your mates, including male and female, especially the wayward ones, are all married and living comfortably with their husbands/wives and you are still there in the house with no ray of hope of settling down now either due to finance (for the men) or because no man has actually come with the issue of marriage (for the ladies)? Were you always having sleepless nights and gnashing your teeth because there is no money to pay for your children's school fees when all were sent home from school? Oh! Is it because you've not made your papers since you started writing WAEC? Is it admission *"palava"* after sitting for JAMB for several years? H-m-m, is it because your in-laws want to get another wife for your husband due to childlessness or because you have not gotten a male child? Is it because your children are giving you trouble day-in-day-out? Is it your neighbours, friends or relations that are causing you heartache and have betrayed you? Then what is it? Mention it. I want you to believe and trust in the Lord who has promised life and not death. Yes, the situation may have changed because the world is really dynamic but God himself has never changed and his faithfulness also remains. He is able to still change that your worst situation for the best. He is the *First* **and the** *Last,* ***the Alpha and the Omega.*** No other king has ever and can ever succeed him. No wonder King Herod and his little-minded nature thought that Jesus Christ was born in order to drag the kingship with him, and that was why he ordered that all the little children born in Bethlehem and its neighbourhood who were two years old and younger should be killed, which was done as recorded in the Gospel of Matthew 2:16. He never knew that Christ is King forever and not a changing God.

However, you can promise and fail, I can promise and fail too. We all have the possibility of not keeping to our words at one point or the other but God has no possibility of disappointing at all. He has promised never to fail us his children and he is always faithful to his words. Isaiah 40:8, GNT says: ***"Yes, grass withers and flowers fade, but the word of our God endures forever"***.

So, do not be afraid of the changing circumstances in the world for the Lord will definitely make uncountable number of ways for you where there is absolutely none as promised.

CHAPTER 3

THE ILLUSION OF LEANING ON TRANSITORY THINGS

I n St. Paul's letter to the Ephesians, husbands and wives were advised to submit themselves to one another because of their reverence for Christ. Specifically, Ephesians 5:22, GNT says: ***"Wives, submit to your husbands as the Lord"***. Verse 25 of the same chapter says: ***"Husbands, love your wives just as Christ loved the church and gave his life for it"***. In other words, husbands and wives are to be committed to themselves in Christ. In Exodus 20:14, the Lord commanded that we should not commit adultery. Based on the above commandment, will you be comfortable to share your lovely wedded wife with another man or your husband with another woman? Definitely, there is no sane person that would be happy with that. Some men/ women are so jealous of their wives/husbands to the extent that they would not even want to see their partner engage in an ordinary conversation with another man/woman talk more of being involved in any illicit behaviour.

Similarly, our God is a jealous God and would not want

to share us, whom he created in his own image and likeness, with other gods. He also commanded us in Exodus 20:5, GNT, thus: *"Do not bow down to any idol or worship it, because I am the Lord your God, and I tolerate no rivals".* I would want you to please recapitulate on these words **"… I am the Lord your God, and I tolerate no rivals".** Our God is indeed a jealous God and would not want to share his glory with anyone/anything. That was the basis for that commandment. Notwithstanding, many of us violate this commandment given to us by God. The truth remains that those other gods can disappoint anyone, anytime, anyhow and anywhere.

In this chapter, the illusion of some of those who leaned on transitory things other than the Most High God was discussed and the outcome shows that most of them received the greatest shock of their lives because disappointment is one of the fruits. Below are some of the examples of those in that category.

3.1   A Lady who Leaned on Her Beauty

There was this lady known as Simora; Simmy for short. To be frank, Simmy was very beautiful; one would say *she was created on the first day of creation when all the materials were still intact.* As aforementioned, Simmy's beauty was an exception. I admired the work of God in her. She was extraordinarily designed. She had a very long hair, fair in complexion (like half-cast), very tall with perfect curves. For a magnet, "like" poles repel (NN or SS) while "unlike poles attract (i.e. North and South). Simmy was a kind of magnet who's "like" and "unlike" poles attract. The domain had no repulsive force at all as she was loved by all.

Simmy was also a sampler. She sampled every new product in the market. She had virtually everything you can think of except

MILLICENT ADANNE CHUKWU

that the means of acquiring them is not enviable at all. She did not mind the categories of people she was dealing with in the course of acquiring money, properties, etc. The only language she understood best was money and she was always ready to offer herself for these material things at anytime, anywhere and with anybody in-so-far-as money is involved. The last thing that Simmy thought about was her Creator; talk more of the after-effects of her way of life. She was completely leaning on her physical beauty. As time rolled by, Simmy's beauty began to fade gradually until she became the shadow of her former self. This was because she suffered from different kinds of disease, which could not be cured. She had been to the best hospitals but all to no avail. At the same time, all her numerous friends abandoned her. Her heart was completely shattered because her body failed her. Simmy finally died mysteriously when her hope, her only source of livelihood, which she was leaning on comfortably disappointed her.

3.2   A Man who Leaned on His Best Friend

Chief Mega was a man who was leaning on his best friend. The chief was very wealthy and had all it takes in making life worthwhile. Before he takes any decision, his friend must be consulted. His wife and children hate such idea but could not help the situation. One day, Chief Mega received a letter from armed robbers, telling him that they will visit him at his residence and that he should keep ten million naira for them. Chief Mega, as usual, consulted his friend who advised him to endeavour to keep the stated amount ready for the robbers and should be away from his premises in order not to be killed. He further advised him not to inform the police because the robbers would seek after his life if they should discover his plans.

However, Chief Mega, after considering that the amount demanded of him was too much and would actually make him skint and as such, thought against keeping such money as demanded. He bought sophisticated guns and was hiding beside his house at night waiting for the D-day. Before then, he had already gone to inform his friend about his new plans but could not meet with him. He then decided to carry out his new plans.

One night, the robbers finally arrived, they were ten in number with the leader in front; on entering the compound, Chief Mega summoned courage, aimed at the leader and shot him down. He also aimed at the second and third and got them down as well. Immediately, the rest ran away. In the morning, behold it was Chief Mega's closest friend who was the leader of the gang. The chief was highly disappointed. He could not believe that his close friend, whom he was leaning on and had much confidence on, could do such. He stared at the corpse with his mouth agape as he too collapsed. Although, he was resuscitated when rushed to the hospital. What a world!

3.3 Corps Members in Camp who Leaned on Some Soldiers/NYSC Officials

On/before 7th of September 2004, most of the 2004 Batch "B" corps members were already at the various NYSC orientation camps all-over the country Nigeria. On that 7th, most of us posted to Cross River State were already in Obubra LGA where the NYSC Orientation Camp was located. The first day was very hectic because everyone was struggling to register. The camp activities started immediately. I discovered that most corps members were worried about where to be posted for their primary assignment. Most people wanted to serve in the city (Calabar). Some even wanted to be in Calabar at all cost. Some corps members were friends with some of the soldiers/NYSC officials just to get their postings influenced. Most of these corps members that were depending on the soldiers/NYSC officials received the greatest shock of their lives when they saw the contrary on their posting letters; during our departure from the camp. Most of these disappointed corps members wept bitterly because their influence did not work. The worst was that most of these officials/soldiers were nowhere to be found after sharing the posting letters. The situation was pure *"OYO"* (On-Your-Own). There was a lady that wept more than others, she was also rolling on the ground and exclaiming *"... after all I did in order to go to Calabar..."*. Only God knows what she involved herself in, so as to be posted to Calabar city, which has failed her. Wa-o-o, human beings and their unpredictable nature!

I have always trusted God in everything and still depended so much on him as regards to my own posting. I had already made up my mind to go to wherever I was posted to as I believe strongly that God would take the lead as always. I gladly accepted my posting to serve in a secondary school in Obudu/Obanliku L.G.A. of Cross River State. My service year in Cross River State was completed successfully as there was no human influence involved. I served in a village that had no light nor water but I was happy for the great success achieved at the end as I won the NYSC State Award to God's glory. Jesus took the lead and I followed, hence, He perfected everything.

3.4 The Family that Leaned on their Children

In the Igbo culture, just as in some other tribes, family members are usually happier when a woman is delivered of a male child than when it is a female child. Women with male children are highly regarded more than those with only female children. Sometimes, people go to the extent of referring to those with female children as not having any child at all. Most times, some of these women with female children are deprived of their rights in the family. May God help us to do away with some of these dehumanizing traditions in our society.

However, there was a woman who had ten sons in a family and she was highly placed. She became the dictator in the family because of her position. Many women envied her, especially those with female children all through. The husband was always fond of her and gives her anything she requested for. The children were pampered to "the point of no return". The parents called them *"Our Soldiers"*. They were healthy looking and strong as well. They indeed look like well-fed soldiers. The mother believed that her problems in life are over with these sons of hers. In their neighbourhood was another woman who had no child. The mother of these ten sons humiliated her to the core and would not allow her children to be of help to the other childless woman in any way. Unknown to the parents, the children joined bad gangs in school. They became chain smokers and drug addicts. Some of these her children are usually involved in any problem that arose in the area. A case of robbery was reported some time ago and four of these children were involved. Unfortunately for the family, they were caught and killed. Out of the five sons that were in the university, three were sentenced to life imprisonment for committing murder in school while two-were rusticated for examination malpractices. The worst is that the parents are now old but have no one to care for them because the last son is still in secondary school while the two that were sent home from school were nowhere to be found. The parents were highly disappointed. They had serious heartache and died mysteriously due to heat failure as they could not withstand the shame brought to them by their own children. No wonder the Bible made us to understand in the book of Proverbs 22:6, that parents should train their children in a good way and these children would never depart from it even when they are old.

3.5   A Man who Leaned on His Wealth

Chief Jad was a very wealthy man. He had uncountable fleet of cars as well as landed properties both within and outside the country. To him, there was no need of going to church because God had already blessed him. The worst was that he dealt with all the poor people around him mercilessly. Some, he snatched their beautiful wives. Those selling close to his shops, he drove away and took over the shares of his business counterparts. He was usually the first to be invited in any occasion because he was very extravagant in his spending and likes showing off. He had some group of friends called *"Otimkpu"* who sings his praises day-in-day-out. Chief Jad was also a very pompous man; always blowing his own trumpet.

However, nemesis caught up with him when the banks he owed came and claimed all he had while he was also detained at the police station because what he even had was not enough to offset his debts. He was able to offset the remaining ones through the help of his in-laws; after which he became *"a nobody"* in the society. All his numerous praise singers disappeared and he is now ashamed of himself because his fleets of cars/properties are no more.

3.6 A Professor who Leaned on His Academic Qualifications/Achievements

"Don't you know me? It is not easy to be a Prof." This is one of the common sayings of one old Professor from one of the famous universities in the country. He believed that he has actually reached the peak and there's none like him as far as academics is concerned. The Prof was really intelligent and had written so many books. He often refers to his certificates as his "life". The old man is the type that does not want his other colleagues to compare with him in any way. He wants to be the only Professor and so he often sits on others' progress by creating one problem or the other for them in order to make sure that they are static in their positions in the office.

The professor was always moving about with his certificates as he uses them to insult others whose levels were still very low. Before you say "Jack Robinson", he brings them out and uses them to insult the hell out of you. That is just to show people that he belonged to many reputable associations and has made it in life academic-wise. One day, he travelled, leaving all his documents in the house. Unfortunately, the house caught fire and all his properties were burnt down, including the certificates. When he came back, he could not withstand the sight of the damage the fire outbreak caused him. He collapsed because he regarded those certificates to be his life.

3.7 A business Man who Leaned on His Charms

Even in this modern time, when Christianity has reached most parts of the world, people still believe in charms. Though we should not be ignorant of the fact that devil still has some powers, but the basic truth remains that our Lord and Saviour Jesus Christ is supreme over all powers.

It is heart wrenching to note that some Christians, baptised, confirmed and some even wedded in the church, believe they cannot make it in life without charms *(Odeshi)*. Some are buried in the houses and shops; some are being hung in hidden places at home and at business areas. Some infuse charms into their bodies in form of marks, etc.

However, there was a man in one market who often boasts of his charms. He was completely leaning on his charms as he consults it and performs incantations before going to his shop every morning. His shop was actually stocked with goods but he just wants to be making extraordinary sales than others around him. As time rolled by, not even flies perched on his goods talk more of anybody coming to price his goods. The man was not happy with the situation but kept it to himself. At the same time, there was one of his neighbours who was making it without charms. He prays always before and after closing from the market, committing his ways to God. The Juju businessman started selling below cost price in order to ensure that he sells at all; notwithstanding, the rush was not there anymore. Most of the perishable goods spoilt while some expired. His capital was seriously affected. At some point, no one was talking of profit again. The cat was let out of the bag when the man brought out a big pot that was buried in his shop for years and broke it outside shouting that it is useless for him despite the amount, he spent in getting the charms. *Wa-o-o!* Instead of the charms to attract more customers for him, the ones he had were even being repelled. After breaking the pot of charms that failed him, he washed his hands off like Pilate did and declared he will not stop serving the Almighty God of his neighbour who is making it.

There are uncountable instances of those who leaned on so many things other than Jesus and were failed woefully. This is just to mention but a few. No wonder the Bible made it clear in the Gospel of John 15:1 – 5, GNT, Jesus says: *"I am the real vine and my father is the gardener. He breaks off every branch in me that does not bear fruit and he prunes every branch that does bear fruit, so that it will be clean and bear more fruit. You have been made clean already by the teaching I have given you. A branch cannot bear fruit by itself; it can do so only if it remains in the vine. In the same way you cannot bear fruit unless you remain in me. I am the vine, and you are the branches. Those who remain in me, and I in them, will bear fruit; for you can do nothing without me."*

Recapitulating on these words *"…. a branch cannot bear fruit by itself; it can only do so if it remains in the vine… for you can do nothing without me."* Is it surprising then that all who were not leaning on Christ were disappointed to the core? Oh! I am not surprised either because our Lord Jesus Christ has categorically stated that we can do absolutely nothing without him being the True Vine. In other words, failing to lean on Christ, the Author and Finisher of our faith is synonymous to failure/ disappointment in life.

Another striking verse in that chapter is verse 7 where Christ says that if you remain in him and his words remain in you, that you shall have anything you ask for. What a privilege! Why do we still lack the basic necessities of life if we can have all we need just by leaning on Christ and asking for it? May the good Lord help us to turn away completely from our old ways of life, which never glorified God's name and return to Jesus Christ, whose arms are wide open to receive us any day, anytime.

CHAPTER 4

THE DIVINE CORRELATION BETWEEN "LEANING ON THE MOST HIGH GOD" AND "VICTORY"

Correlation is the degree of relationship existing between two or more variables. "Leaning on the Most High" and "Victory" are two variables that are dichotomous in nature because they cannot be measured quantitatively. Notwithstanding, these two variables are perfectly positively correlated because I have never seen or heard of anyone who depends on God sincerely and wholeheartedly and was failed; rather, victory was always their watchword. I can say without mincing words that the degree of correlation between these two variables is likely to be equal to *one;* which is the highest degree of correlation because our God is perfect in all sense of the word. Due to the fact that none of the modern econometric techniques would be employed in this case to carry out all the necessary tests, the testimonies/true life experiences of some of those who leaned on God and were favoured are recorded as proofs instead.

4.1 Some Women who were Blessed after Several years of Childlessness

God is a perfect planner and a perfect designer. The Lord reassures us of his wonderful plans for us in Jeremiah 29:11, GNT, which says *"I alone know the plan I have for you, plans to bring you prosperity and not disaster, plans to bring about the future you hoped for."*

It is never the plan of God to deprive any family the wonderful blessing of children. The Lord stated it clearly in Genesis 1:27 – 28, GNT, which says: *"So God created human beings, making them to be like himself. He created them male and female, blessed them and said, have many children so that your descendants will live all over the earth and bring it under their control."*

There are so many other promises of God for us through his word, which is life in itself and would be discussed in subsequent chapters. Remember that our God can do and undo but one thing that God cannot do is that he cannot lie. The Lord honours his words more than his name. He is indeed the God that fulfils promises. The big question that someone may ask is: *"Why is it that so many families today are suffering from childlessness even among dedicated Christians?* So many factors could be responsible for this but whatever the reason(s), the fact remains that God has never and can never fail anyone who puts his trust in him.

However, there was a woman who lived with her husband for good 20 years without any child. She was always crying to God just as Hannah did during her time. Her heart was always skipping when she reached the age of menopause. The people of God were always around her and encouraging her and she continued trusting God. She never loosed hope not minding that she was ageing seriously. The kind of insult she had received on several occasions from the in-laws, neighbours, friends, relations, etc. is nothing to write home about. She was always crying her heart out to God. After about 20 years of marriage, God answered her prayers and dried her tears by blessing her with two children, a boy and a girl even when she had exceeded her menopause stage in life. Surely, there is nothing like menopause in the dictionary of God.

In addition, Jackie Mize, the author of *"supernatural Childbirth"* was told by her doctor that she cannot have any child in her life, though she did not state the reason(s) for the statement but she told the husband what the doctor said when he proposed to her. The husband, Terry L. Mize, being a man of faith, on hearing that, replied: *"Oh, I see. Well, God said you can have babies, even though I thank God for doctors and hospitals, and medical science is always advancing, they are not our final source, our final authority – God – is, and God said you can have children."* The man's faith in God saw him through. He went ahead and married her irrespective of the doctor's report. God glorified himself in their lives by blessing them with four children: Lynn, Paul, Lori and Cristy. God indeed makes ways where there is absolutely none. To him alone be all the glory.

Furthermore, in Genesis 17:15 – 19, GNT, God said to Abraham, ***"You must no longer call your wife Sarai from now on, her name is Sarah. I will bless her and I will give you a son by her. I will bless her and she will become the mother of nations, and there will be kings among her descendants"***. Abraham bowed down with his face touch the ground but he began to laugh when he thought, *"Can a man have a child when he is a hundred years old? Can Sarah have a child at ninety?"* So, Abraham requested that Ishmael should be his heir, but God refused and told him that his wife Sarah will bear him a son, which he will name Isaac.

In Genesis 18: 1 – 14, GNT, the Lord also appeared to Abraham at the sacred trees of Mamre in form of three men. Abraham was sitting at the entrance of his tent during the hottest part of the day when he saw the three men standing there. Bowing down with his face touching the ground, he pleaded that they should not pass by his home without stopping. He offered them some water to wash their feet; served them food and they ate in order to rest before continuing with their journey. They asked after his wife and one of them said: *"Nine months from now, I will come back, and your wife Sarah will have a son"*. Sarah was at the door of the tent, listening and laughed to herself on hearing this because they were very old and she had even stopped having her monthly periods. Then the Lord asked Abraham, *"Why did Sarah laugh and say, 'can I really have a child when I am so old?" is anything too hard for the Lord? As I said, nine months from now I will return and Sarah will have a son."* God is indeed the God that fulfils promises as all these came to pass at exactly the period, which the Lord foretold.

Oh! Reflect on verse 14: *"… Is anything too hard for the Lord?"* There is absolutely nothing that is hard, talk more of too hard for the Lord. He is the God of possibilities, who does not change but changes all kind of circumstances. He is the Hope of the hopeless, the joy of the sorrowful, and the comfort of the afflicted. God is the Almighty and All-Powerful God. Are you married for many years without children, which are a gift from the Lord and a real blessing as recorded in Psalm

127:3? Are you and your husband too old that no one expects anything like children from you again? Have you reached the age of menopause and all your hope of having children lost? Have you been having countless miscarriage that not even one child could stay in your womb? Did your doctor tell you that you could never have any child in your life? Were you told that you have no womb or that you have got a damaged womb? Were you told that your womb has been removed spiritually even when it is physically there? Were you told that you are not man enough to impregnate a woman? Were you told that someone is responsible for your inability to have children? What is your case like? Whatever the case may be, I just want you to always have in mind that there is absolutely nothing that is difficult for our Lord to do. The Lord says in Psalm 46:10 that you should be still and know that he is God, supreme among the nations, supreme over the world. The Lord will be your fertility in Jesus' name, Amen. He will definitely give you hope as he did to Abraham and Sarah. He will wipe away your hot tears and make you proud to the glory of his name. Continue to lean on God and look up to him for help just as a servant depends on his master and a maid depends on her mistress (Psalm 123).

The most important of whatever is said about you is what God says. Yes, the doctors have said theirs, those who see tomorrow you have visited, said theirs. Your enemies have also said theirs, but the most important of all is what God says. God says that you can have children. Claim it in Jesus' name. Behold God's promise to you in Psalm 128:3, GNT; *"Your wife will be like a fruitful vine in your home, and your children will be like young olive trees round your table"*. Matthew 10:28, ESV says: *"Do not be afraid of those who kill the body but cannot kill the soul; fear him rather who can destroy both body and soul in hell"*. If you feel that anybody locked your womb and that is why you've not been able to conceive, please calm your fears and have confidence that our Lord and Saviour Jesus Christ can unlock it and restore your fertility. As aforementioned in Genesis 18:14, GNT, *"Is there anything too hard for the Lord?"* None at all! Your age does not matter because there is absolutely nothing like menopause in the dictionary of God. What matters is your trust in God; so, do not ever limit God's ability. He will turn the darkness in your life into God's wonderful light in Jesus' name, Amen.

Furthermore, Elkanah had two wives, Hannah and Peninnah, as recorded in 1 Samuel 1:1 – 28, GNT. Peninnah had children but the Lord kept Hannah from having children and as a result, Peninnah tormented and humiliated Hannah to the extent that she would be crying and refuse to eat anything. One day, after they had finished their meal in the house of the Lord at Shilo, Hannah got up and was deeply distressed. She cried bitterly to God as she prayed. She made a solemn promise to the Lord as follows:

> *"Almighty Lord, look at me, your servant! See my trouble and remember me! Don't forget me! If you give me a son, I promise that I will dedicate him to you for his whole life and that he will never have his hair cut".*

Eli the priest accused Hannah of being drunk but she told him plainly that she was just praying and pouring out her troubles to the Lord. Then Eli said to her: *"Go in peace and may the God of Israel give you what you have asked him for."* The Lord actually heard her prayers by blessing her with Samuel. She in turn fulfilled her own promise by taking Samuel, young as he was, to the house of the Lord at Shilo; just after she had weaned him. She met Eli and said to him; *"Excuse me Sir, do you remember me? I am the woman you saw standing here, praying to the Lord, I asked him for this child, and he gave me what I asked for. So, I am dedicating him to the Lord. As long as he lives, he will belong to the Lord"*.

May the good Lord who granted Hannah what she asked for bless you with children to the glory of his name in Jesus' name, Amen! Don't ever lose hope for the Lord is very much able to do it for you.

Genesis 30:22 – 24, GNT: *"Then God remembered Rachel; he answered her prayer and made it possible for her to have children. She became pregnant and gave birth to a son. She said, God has taken away my disgrace by giving me a son. May the Lord give me another son"*.

My dear families of God who are still looking unto God for the wonderful fruits of the womb; I am claiming Hannah and Rachael's portion for you and praying that the Almighty God who remembered Hannah, answered her prayer and made it possible for her to have children will remember you, answer your prayers and make it possible for you to have children too in Jesus name; Amen. God hears and answers prayers. The Bible tells us in Psalm 37:4 that we should seek our happiness from the Lord and he will give us the desires of our heart. Husband and wife should be in agreement with themselves and at the same time with the word of God, pray with the word always, which is life in itself. Wives should always believe and desire to conceive because this is one of the greatest fulfilments over barrenness.

Moreover, the Lord has declared that none shall be barren in the land (Exodus 23: 26, GNT). *"In your land, no woman will have miscarriage or be without children. I will give you long lives"*. Also, Deuteronomy 7:13 – 14 GNT says: *"He will love you and bless you so that you will increase in number and have many children no people in the world will be as richly blessed as you. None of you nor any of your livestock will be sterile (barren).* Psalm 113:9, GNT says: *"He honours the childless wife in her home; he makes her happy by giving her children".*

I would want us to realize the fact that sometimes, God purposely prevents some people from having children but when he remembers them, he still enables them to have their own kids; just as in the case of Sarah, Hannah and Rachael. Take a look at the following quotations:

- Genesis 16:12, GNT – Sarah said: *"... and the Lord has kept me from having children".*
- Genesis 29:31, GNT – *"When the Lord saw that Leah was loved less than Rachel, he made it possible for her to have children but Rachel remained childless."*
- Genesis 30:1 – 2, GNT – *"But Rachel had not borne Jacob any children and so she became jealous of her sister and said to Jacob, give me children or I will die. Jacob became angry with Rachel and said, I can't take the place of God. He is the one who keeps you from having children."*
- 1 Sam 1:19, GNT – *"... and the Lord answered her prayers. So it was that she became pregnant and gave birth to a son..."*

From the above few quotations, it is very obvious that sometimes, God himself purposely allow some families to be childless before eventually blessing them at his own time. All are to the glory of his name. **my dear in the Lord, how then can someone who has lived a very careless life in his or her youthful age be sure that his or her inability of having children when married is of God?** This is an intricate issue with special concern because I have once overhead a girl telling her friend that she cannot recall how many times she had committed abortion in life talk more of the number of times she had taken contraceptives. This, of course, is very dangerous and many people have lost their lives as a result. If for instance such a person gets married without issues for some years, she may not be certain whether it is God who is preventing her from having children or it is as a result of the uncountable number of abortions committed when single. Guilt may not even allow her to pray and challenge God as supposed because of these uncertainties. This is the more reason why I want to encourage my fellow young ladies and men as well so that we may try as much as possible through the grace of God to live a decent and holy life in our youthful age for a brighter future. I am not disputing the fact that God is full of mercy, he can forgive all sins and can even restore your damaged womb. There are people who have lived a very rough life before yet are blessed with many children today. Remember that in James, we are asked whether we can remain in sin so that grace may abound? The answer is capital *"NO"*.

However, if you are still looking unto God for the gift of children and you have nothing to regret about your past, please continue to pray for God will surely remember you as he did to Sarah, Rachel and Hannah, etc. Even if you have a lot to regret about your past life, do not worry still, just remember what is written in II Corinthians 5:17, GNT – *"Anyone who is joined to Christ is a new being; the old is gone, the new has come"*. In so-far-as you have turned away completely from your old way of life and living sincerely in Christ, he will definitely forgive you and change your situation because he is able to do all things. II Chronicle 7:14, GNT crowned it all as follows:

"If they pray to me and repent and turn away from the evil they have been doing, then I will hear them in heaven, forgive their sins and make their land prosperous again". Praise the Lord!

4.2 Elijah and the Prophets of Baal (1 Kings 18: 1 – 40, GNT)

Looking at the case between Prophet Elijah and the 450 prophets of Baal, we can see that the bone of contention was when Jezebel was killing the Lord's prophets, Obadiah who was a devout worshiper of the Lord took a hundred of them and hid in caves in two groups of 50. He provided them with food and water. On his way to find enough grass to keep the horses and mules alive, he met with Elijah. Elijah asked Obadiah to go and tell his master that he is around but Obadiah refused for fear of being killed by the King. Elijah then decided to present himself to the King, which he did.

Elijah requested that all the people of Israel should meet him at Mount Carmel; that they should bring along the 450 prophets of Baal and the 400 prophets of the goddess Asherah who are supported by Queen Jezebel. When this was done, Elijah went up to the people and said:

"How much longer will it take you to make up your minds? If the Lord is God, worship him; but if Baal is God, worship him! I am the only prophet of the Lord still left, but there are 450 prophets of Baal. Bring two bulls, let the Prophets of Baal take one, kill it, cut it in pieces, and put it on the wood – but don't light the fire. I will do the same with the other bull. Then let the prophets of

Baal pray to their god and I will pray to the Lord, and the one who answers by sending fire – he is God." The people agreed to that and Elijah asked the prophets of Baal to take a bull and prepare it first since they were many. They took the bull that was brought to them, prepared it and prayed to Baal until noon but there was no answer. They were even dancing round the altar they had built and were shouting that Baal should answer them but there was no answer at all.

At noon, Elijah started making fun of them by saying: *"Pray louder! He is a god! Maybe he is daydreaming or relieving himself or perhaps he's gone on a journey! Or maybe he's sleeping and you've got to wake him up!"* So, the prophets prayed louder and cut themselves with knives and daggers, according to their ritual until blood flowed. They kept on ranting and raving until the middle of the afternoon, but no answer came, not even a sound was heard. Elijah then told the people to come close to him and they did. He repaired the altar of the Lord, which was torn down with twelve stones, one for each of the twelve tribes of Israel. Elijah also dug a trench round the altar, large enough to hold almost 14 litres of water. Then he placed the wood on the altar, cut the bull in pieces and laid it on the wood. He asked them to fill four jars with water and pour it on the offering and the wood. He further asked them to do it two more times, which was done. The water ran down round the altar and filled the trench.

At the hour of the afternoon sacrifice, Prophet Elijah approached the altar and prayed, *"O Lord, the God of Abraham, Isaac and Jacob, prove now that you are the God of Israel and that I am your Servant and have done all this at your command.*

Answer me, Lord, answer me, so that this people will know that you, the Lord are God, and that you are bringing them back to yourself".

The Lord sent fire down and it burn up the sacrifice, the wood and the stones, scorched the earth and dried up the water in the trench. When the people saw this, they threw themselves on the ground and exclaimed, *"The Lord is God, the Lord alone is God."*

We can see clearly that the Most High God whom Elijah was leaning on did not fail him unlike that of the prophets of Baal. What are you leaning on as God/god? That god tied on your waist, under your pillow, inside your pocket, in form of marks on your body or as rings has neither ears nor mouth and cannot assist you. The devil, of course, has no free gift for you, his gift is on *"give and take"* basis. He will give you little and take more in return. It is our Lord and Saviour Jesus Christ that can give you free gifts. The Israelites, after seeing what God did through Prophet Elijah, took the immediate decision to serve the Living God. What about you? I pray that the wonderful God of Elijah will help you make the right choice **NOW** in Jesus name; Amen.

4.3   The Israelites Crossed the Red Sea

When the Israelites were departing from Egypt to the promised land as recorded in Exodus 14:1 – 29, GNT, the Pharaoh's heart was hardened and he set out with all is chariots, including the 600 finest, commanded by their officers. He pursued the Israelites who were leaving triumphantly. The Egyptian army with all the horses, chariots and drivers caught up with the Israelites who were camped by the Red Sea. When the Israelites saw the King and his army marching against them, they were terrified and cried out to the Lord for help. The Israelites also attacked Moses that it would be better for them to continue to be slaves in Egypt than to die in the desert. Moses answered, *"Don't be afraid! Stand your ground and you will see what the Lord will do to save you today; the Egyptians you see today, you shall see no more. The Lord will fight for you and there is need for you to do anything."* The Lord then commanded Moses to lift his stick and hold it out over the sea and the Lord drove the sea back with a strong east wind. It blew all night and turned the sea into dry land. The Lord also protected the Israelites with the pillar of cloud by day and the pillar of fire by night.

However, as the water divided, the Israelites went through the sea on dry ground, with walls of water on both sides. The Egyptians pursued them and went after them into the sea with all their horse, chariots and drivers. The Lord threw them into a panic and made the wheels of their chariots get stock, so that they moved with great difficulty. The Egyptians said; *"The Lord is fighting for the Israelites against us. Let's get out of here!"* Then the Lord told Moses to hold out his hand over the sea and Moses held out his hand over the sea and the water returned to its normal level. The Egyptians tried to escape from the water but the Lord threw them into the sea. The water covered the chariots, the drivers and all the Egyptian army that had followed the Israelites into the sea. Not one of them was left; but the Israelites walked through the sea on dry ground, with walls of water on both sides. When the Israelites saw this marvellous work of the Lord, they had faith in God.

Our God is indeed a faithful God. He is ever faithful to us even when we are unfaithful. Then imagine God's faithfulness when we try to exhibit our own atom of faithfulness. As aforementioned severally, God has never and can never fail anyone who leans on him. God does not change at all. He protected the Israelites from the hands of their enemies. He will also deliver you from those Egyptians of our time that are troubling you. Those Egyptians in your village that would not allow you to progress in anything you do, those Egyptians in your compound as neighbours, those Egyptians in your place of work that are sitting tight on your promotion, those Egyptians in your school that would not allow you to graduate because you have refused to sell your birth-right as a child of God, those Egyptians as relatives that are trying to claim all your husband's properties because he's late, those Egyptians of physical and spiritual backwardness, the Egyptians of late marriages even when you are trying to live a holy life as a child of God, the Egyptians of childlessness even when the doctors have declared that you and your partner are alright, the Egyptian in your life, I declare with the power in the precious Blood of Jesus Christ of Nazareth that you shall see those Egyptians no more in your life; amen. The Lord who fought for the Israelites is able to fight for you. Just continue to lean on him with all sincerity at all times; he will definitely wipe away your hot tears and make it possible for you to laugh louder to the glory of his name.

4.4 A Lady who Refused to Sell Her Birth Right While Searching for job

Life is not always a bed of roses; even roses have some element of thorns. The thorns are not the major problem but how one is able to handle them matters a lot. Leaning on our Lord Jesus Christ gives the strength and the wisdom to overcome any kind of temptation that comes on one's way. Remember what is written in the Gospel of John 15:15, GNT – *"I am the vine and you are the branches... for you can do nothing without me"*.

The psalmist says that good people suffer many troubles but the Lord delivers them from all their troubles.

There was this lady who was searching for work after many years of graduation. She believed so much in the Lord and leaned on him sincerely that she commits all her ways to God. It was not as though there was no offer of appointment at all but the major issue was that there were many strings attached in each case; which were never to the glory of God. She holds herself to a high esteem, knowing fully well that her body is the temple of the Holy Spirit. As a result, she lost most of the job opportunities she got because of her refusal to offer herself as a *"dead sacrifice"* to those men who were out to take advantage of poor innocent girls and mar their relationship with God. She stood her ground irrespective of all the agonies she passed through in trying to manage her life as a lady. She did not lose hope either; but continued to pray and cry to God concerning her condition. The Lord, of course, heard her cry and made it possible for her to get appointment in a reputable company without any condition attached this time around. The Lord further blessed her with a wonderful husband and two kids now she has an enviable family to the glory of God. Praise the Lord! Indeed, God's delay is not his denial. At the appointed time, the Lord will surely see you through too in Jesus name, amen.

4.5   A Man's Damaged Heart was Restored

There was also a man who had heart disease and had been taken to good hospitals with qualified doctors and nurses but his case got worst to the extent that the doctors had already predicted how long the man would live on earth. The man is a child of God and did not lose hope despite the fact that the doctors and nurses were already tired of his case. While in the hospital, his Parish Priest always visits him, prays for him and gives him the Holy Eucharist each time he visits. The God of miracle manifested himself in the life of that man by making it possible for a new heart to develop and replaced the damaged heart. When the doctors examined him, they noticed that a new heart had already replaced the old one; they were astonished and then discharged the man. They went home with joy and were testifying this everywhere to the glory of God.

How long have you been in the hospital? What is your case like? Are the doctors and nurses tired of taking care of your ill health? Is there no hope of being healed again? Whatever your case may be, my dear in the Lord, do not despair. Jesus is able to do it for you. He begins his wonderful works when all hope is lost. He is our Last Resort. He did it for the above-mentioned man and to others in many places; he will do it for you too. He is the same yesterday, today and forever; the Lord promised that healing shall be his children's daily bread; I claim that for you in the name of Jesus, Amen. Our God is the God that fulfils promises. He further says that by his stripes that we are healed. May you continue to be healed through the stripes of our Lord in Jesus name, Amen! The wounded Messiah will do it for you. He is the Hope of the hopeless, the Healing Messiah, the unchangeable Changer, the Beginning and the End. The doctors have said theirs but what matters most is what God says about you. I am happy to announce the good news of the Lord to you today; the Lord says that you shall live to testify his goodness in the land of the living. Just continue to lean on the Lord, have faith that he can do it and see it done. God's ways and thoughts differ from ours. A thousand years is like a day in the sight of God and vice versa. I pray that the wounded Messiah will touch you on the sick bed with his mighty healing hands and make you whole in the name of Jesus, amen. I cover you with the Blood and water which gushes forth from the sides of the Lord; may they pass through your veins and arteries and begin to correct every abnormality in your system in the name of Jesus, Amen. Thank Jesus because I trust he has done it already for you since we pray through Jesus Christ our Lord; Amen.

4.6 A Student and Her Project Supervisor/Lecturer

This is another true-life testimony of a student from one of the Nigerian Universities whose lecturer/project supervisor threatened because she refused to yield to his selfish requests. The lecturer taught them a total of 9-credit unit load (a course of 3 credit unit and the project which is 6 credit unit). One day, the lady brought part of her project work for supervision into his office and he wanted to touch her unduly but the lady being a good Christian repelled him and told him that she is already engaged. The lecturer then said that he too is married and as such, equation has balanced. The lecturer insisted that they get involved in an illicit affair but the lady stood her ground and refused. The lecturer reminded her that her 9-credit unit load was in his hands, except if she wouldn't want to graduate with her mates she then walked away, crying bitterly and met me and narrated the whole story to me; that the man had threatened her on several occasions before that day. I felt for her and then encouraged her to have faith that God is able to vindicate her. As a result, we went into fasting and prayers for days concerning the issue. After one week, she went back to present part of her project to him and the lecturer did not mention anything stupid again. The Lord indeed favoured her and she graduated with her mates without any issue. She is now happily married with a beautiful baby girl; whose name is Divine.

Are you still in school and passing through any kind of difficult situation in the hands of your lecturers or project supervisor? Do not worry! Commit it to God and God who answered my friend as aforesaid will do it for you. The way you live your life generally matters a lot my dear, especially my fellow young ladies. What would you ask God to do to your lecturer who is tormenting you and has given you many carry-overs, prevented you from graduating with your mates because you have refused to sleep with him when you are in turn living a dirty life within and outside the campus? Remember the Scripture says in Galatians 6:7, GNT – *"Do not deceive yourselves, no one makes a fool of God. People will reap exactly what they sow"*. If you try as much as possible through the grace of God which is sufficient for us to live a holy life, especially by avoiding this sin of immorality which is the order of the day in our society. I believe strongly that God will never fail to vindicate you from the hands of whosoever that wants to tamper with you for refusing to commit this sin with him/her. Yes, you may suffer along the line but God will definitely make a way out for you. Actually, there are other kinds of sin which are also grievous and can mar our relationship with God but I would love to share with you what the scripture says in I Corinthians 6:18, GNT: *"Avoid immorality any other sin a man commits does not affect his body; but the man who is guilty of sexual immorality sins against his own body. Don't you know that your body is the temple of the Holy Spirit, who lives in you and who was given to you by God? You do not belong to yourselves but to God; he bought you for a price. So, use your bodies for God's glory"*.

Our body is indeed the Temple of the Holy Spirit and we are worth more than gold. We are precious in the sight of God who lives in us and engaging ourselves in anything silly will mar our relationship with God and at the same time be great stumbling block to our progress in life. It beats my imagination when I hear people say that they cannot sleep even for one day without a man or a woman; especially among the unmarried youth. I've heard one who mentioned in school that no one can ever boast of that. In logic, this is called *"faulty generalization";* and this is one of the strategies that the devil is using to strengthen those he has captured; to feel that everybody is involved, which is not true at all. God created us and made us to have control over every other thing he created on earth including our bodies but the issue is that some are rather being controlled by their bodies/emotions. My dearest in the Lord, you can do without anything you can think of in this life except Christ. Remember his words in John 15:5, ESV – *"for apart from me, you can do nothing".* It is only our Lord and Saviour Jesus Christ that we cannot do without. *It is not by power, nor by might but by my spirit, says the Lord.* Decide today, lean on Christ and he will give you the grace to overcome and subdue those bad habits that you feel you cannot do without. I pray that the good Lord will give you the abundant grace needed as you take the drastic decision to change positively to the glory of God in the name of Jesus; amen.

4.7 My True-Life Experience (The Author)

This book would not be complete if I fail to share part of my testimonies and the faithfulness of God in my life. I mean part because God has done so much in my life that even the whole book cannot contain all if they are to be documented.

On the 10th of January 2000, I went to the University of Abuja to check whether my name was short-listed on the first list of admission that pasted on the notice board. When I discovered that my name was not on the list, I just went to one of the hostels and stayed with Christy Ezenwaka who was in her final year then. While with her, I bought some books and started lectures because I wouldn't want to miss anything before my name comes out (Just being hopeful and trusting God). I applied for Computer Science, as my first and second choice. I was optimistic that my name would be out with the second list but behold, my name was not there when the list eventually came out. I wept bitterly, but did not lose hope at all. I believe that God can do it for me but do not know how because I knew nobody in that University then to physically help me in that regard. I joined the Nigerian Federation of Catholic Students (NFCS) and participated actively in the group, paid all my dues even without admission then. I was also participating actively in the department, attended lectures religiously, and wrote all the assignments and tests given without admission still. While these were going on, I was always visiting the Blessed Sacrament at St. Paul's Catholic Church, Phase-Three, Gwagwalada, Abuja, very close to the University of Abuja. I was always crying to God, fasting and praying, reminding him of all his promises to me. I clung unto God so tightly for help believing he will not fail me. After the second list came out without my name still, I began to make declarations that the third list will never come out until my name enters the list. Although, I do not know how my name would be included in the list but was just trusting and believing the God of miracle who could do all things.

However, on the 29th of January 2000, the Lord remembered me and actually included my name on the third list. I wanted to study Computer Science but God who knows the best for me chose Economics for me. I did not spend any money for admission's sake; the Lord gave it to me freely.

The Lord did not stop at that, he saw me through in all

my endeavours while at the University of Abuja, provided all I needed and helped me to graduate as the best student both in the department of Economics and the faculty of social sciences. All to the glory of His name. God did not stop there still, as I have been asked to resume work as a lecturer in the department of Economics as a result of my outstanding performance, which was made possible by God himself, the lifter of the lowly. I will resume work at the end of this service year as a graduate assistant and I ask the good Lord who has made this possible to please, continue to be in perfect control.

Are you still looking for admission into the university and you feel you have no connection and money to get there? Do not worry o-o-! The same God that did it for me will surely see you through as well. He will give you hope and make ways for you where there is absolutely none. Do not lose hope at all; continue to lean on God. He never fails and can never fail you.

Surely, there is a divine correlation between "leaning on the Most High God" and "Victory" because all the people testified above were able to succeed through the grace of God whom they were leaning on for help.

I pray that whatever your need may be, the God that does not change will also manifest himself in your life to his glory. Do not be tired of waiting/trusting on the Lord patiently for his delay is never his denial. He will see you through at his own appointed time. He would surely make you laugh last, laugh louder/longer and laugh best. I am a living testimony.

CHAPTER 5

THE DEVICES OF THE DEVIL

T he devil already knows where he belongs and would not want to remain there alone. He wants many followers and that is why he mapped out many strategies with which to deceive people into doing things that are contrary to the will of God. There are so many things we do or say in this world today which does not matter to us but matters in the real sense. Some of these strategies are manifested in the following slogans we use today in our society.

- *"The Bible says we should enjoy ourselves while we are still young"*
- *"After all, everybody is involved"*
- *"If you cannot beat them, you join them"*
- *"Go and sleep with another man, you may be pregnant so that you can prove to the world that you are innocent of what your husband's family are saying about you".*
- *"Nothing can ever be good again"*
- *"There is still more time to repent after enjoying one's life"*
- *"After all, God created it in us!"*

- *"We are just human beings"*
- *"No one is righteous, the Bible says"*
- *"We are in the modern age, the jet/computer age and not in the Stone Age".*
- *"It does not matter"* syndrome and the like.

These and many other assumptions are some of the mapped-out strategies the devil uses to keep some people in perpetual bondage. Some scriptural passages are often misinterpreted; like that of the psalmist, which says that we should enjoy ourselves while we are still young; yes, enjoyment is good but *"how?"* is the very big question. If God is being glorified in our activities in life and at the same time, maximum satisfaction is being derived, then we can continue, but if God is not glorified in any kind of activity we engage in even if our flesh is being satisfied, it is never enjoyment. I do refer to such activities as *"enjoy-death"*. Though we know that death is not even enjoyable at all even when we are aware of the fact that our mortal bodies would be transformed before getting to our final destination – **Heaven;** and that is why people weep bitterly and not laughing when they lose their loved ones. However, as youths, we are supposed to give more time to the things of God while we are still young and strong. The greatest of all kinds of enjoyment is gotten in Christ. Outside Christ, enjoyment is equal to zero and sometimes, tends towards negative. Remember that we cannot be young forever as recorded in **Ecclesiastes 11:9-10** GNT which says "Young people, enjoy your youth. Be happy while you are still young. Do what you want to do, and follow your heart's desire. But remember that God is going to judge you for whatever you do. Don't let anything worry you or cause you pain. You aren't going to be young very long"

Another strategy that the evil one uses is the assumption that

"... everyone is involved after all"; this is not true at all because there are exceptions. It is another case of faulty generalization mentioned previously. Due to this belief, people tend to remain in their evil/bad ways, rather than making a total "U"-turn. Even during the time of Sodom and Gomorrah, God was able to single out Lot and his family out of that corrupt city. Notwithstanding that our country is full of evil, bribery and corruption being the order of the day, most of our higher institutions are full of social vices, etc. There are still exceptions but it is only the All-Knowing God, who sees in secret that knows all. It is high time we stop using the *slangs* that all are involved in backing up or strengthening ourselves in our evil/ wrong ways of life. Remember that we are indeed in the world but not of the world. I pray that the good Lord will give us the strength to remain faithful to him even while still in this sinful world; in Jesus name, Amen.

Gone are the days when you join a particular group if you cannot beat them. That has enslaved many, especially in our higher institutions where many students who came from good homes are being carried away by so many negative activities in school because they believe so much on the slogan. I believe strongly in segregating yourself if you cannot beat them. Remember, your friends matter a lot in life. It is usually said that if you show me your friend, I will tell you whom you are. The Bible made it clearer in 1 Corinthians 15:33 – 34, GNT; *"Do not be fooled, bad companion ruins good character. Come back to your right senses and stop your sinful ways...".* If you have friends with questionable character, try as much as you can to help them through prayers, advice and encouragement to change for good, if possible to change for the best; but if you cannot, instead of being part, please do segregate yourself completely in order not to be influenced negatively. I pray that the good Lord will help us to keep good companions through which his name might be glorified.

"Nothing can ever be good again; we are just human beings after all; God created it in us, the bible even says that no one is righteous…" The above statements and the like are also part of the strategies the evil ones use to achieve their aims. We should be optimistic in our ways of reasoning because we are people of hope. The fact that the situation of things is not favourable sometimes does not mean that it can never be better again. Some people capitalize on it while carrying out their act of wickedness. They are not thinking of repentance at all since they believe that nothing good can ever come out of the world again. It's quite true, the world and its contents are dynamic but God remains unchangeable as discussed in chapter two. There is absolutely nothing difficult for our God to do. He can change all situations but cannot change. Since we are people of hope, it is therefore better we continue to be optimistic and also try to improve in our relationship with God at all times.

However, the issue of *"… being human and God creating it in us as well as the Bible saying that none is righteous"* should not be used as a pillar to lean on while digressing from the ways of God. In the book of James, we were asked if we should continue in sin so that grace may abound? The answer remains *"NO"*. The grace of God is over sufficient for us. Our God is full of mercy and is ever ready to receive us back like the prodigal son in the gospel of St. **Luke 15:11-32**; if only we can take the decision to change positively and continue to lean on him all the days of our lives.

There was a day one of my friends' Ojinika Amadi and I went for all-night browsing in a Cyber Café opposite our university gate to do one of our assignments. We got a mail that night whose content is on how the devil struggles to weigh down the children of God through diverse means. One of those ways is to make sure that people are very much engaged with worldly activities and so have little or no time for God. Coincidentally, there was a "Divine Mercy" programme, which involves the exposition of the Blessed Sacrament at St. Paul's Catholic Church, Gwagwalada, Abuja; for nine hours the next morning. The major issue then was that we were awake till about 6.00 a.m. in the morning and I was already exhausted to attend the church programme, which I was very much aware of before going for the all-night browsing. My spirit was very willing to go but my flesh was completely weak so I thought of going to the hostel to have my rest. Immediately, the devil's strategy that was mailed to me flashed through my mind and I changed my mind. I then prayed for God to give me the strength to attend the Divine Mercy nine hours devotion, and he actually did. I went and participated actively during the programme to the glory of God till we dismissed.

When we are conscious of the devil's tricks, we will hardly fall into his traps by God's grace. A problem known is said to be a problem half-solved. Since we know that the evil ones are never at rest, we Christians are supposed to be alert at all times.

During one of the national conventions of the National Association of Catholic Corps Members (NACC) held at Enugu, Rev. Fr Emmanuel Onuh, during his speech, told us that the devil uses three basic strategies to pull believers away from God. The first is that the devil tries as much as possible to distract you from the things/ways of God. If he succeeds, he will go further to attract you with some gold-looking things after which he goes further to contract you to work in his vineyard. May God forbid that in Jesus name, Amen. Our Lord and Saviour Jesus Christ will rather contract us to work fervently in his vineyard. All we need to do is to make ourselves available for the Lord. He has endowed us all with different kinds of gifts. May God help us to discover our individual gifts and utilise them efficiently to the glory of God; Amen.

Furthermore, you must be ready to make Jesus Christ the number one in your life in order not to be distracted by the evil one. Allow him to guide and guard you. Study the word of God meticulously at all times because the great power in the **Word** breaks every yoke. So many things are happening in this world that we should continue to be steadfast. We must glue ourselves tight to our Lord Jesus Christ in order not to be distracted by any of the activities that are taking place in the world today

It is pertinent to note that the devil will not contract you if you are not attracted at all. For you not to be attracted, you must be contented with whatever your parents are able to provide for you while in school. Be contended with what you have and God will expand your horizon as you keep working harder and trusting in Him. No matter how ugly/hopeless your situation may be, God is able to change your story for the best if you ask of him; see the Gospel of **Matthew 7:7.**

Everything in life is not all about money, though money is quite good but always have in mind that money is not everything. Some students are usually being distracted and attracted by the evil one due to their inability to live according to their family's income level. Some are living false life on campus and want to have every new product in the market in order to belong. Some mothers fall into this category as well because they want to look like *the happening* women in the society without putting into consideration their own husband's source of income. The evil one also distracts some young guys because they want to meet up with their mates. No matter the category you find yourself, the bottom line remains that the devil will not distract, attract or contract you when you tend to be very contented with whatever God has blessed you with. If he does even when you are satisfied with what you have, the Lord will definitely give you the ability to overcome. Appreciate God for whom you are and let everything about you glorify the name of God. Be very hardworking because to work is to pray as well, and God will not fail to bless the works of your hands and enlarge your coast. Above all, seek first the kingdom of God and his righteousness and every other thing you need shall be added unto you (**Matthew 6:33, ESV**). This is one of the promises of God who does not fail, not even in his words. Remember the case of Solomon who asked God for wisdom alone and the Lord not only gave him wisdom but granted him wealth as well. Our case will not be different because that God of Solomon, Elijah, Abraham, Isaac and Jacob cannot change in our time. He is still our God. Remember too that your hard work alone without Christ is equal to zero. Some are rich not just because they work harder than others while some that are still poor does not mean that they are lazy. It is God that gives wealth/riches without any string attached. He is able to make a poor man instantly rich and vice versa. I am not disputing the fact that we also have our own part to play in order that the wonderful plans that God has for us will come to fulfilment. The point I am trying to buttress is that we cannot succeed on our own without Christ, the true Vine (**Jn. 15:1-7**).

However, in the book of Job 2:1 – 2, GNT, it is written that when the day came for the heavenly beings to appear before the Lord, that Satan was there among them; when the Lord asked him where he had been, he answered ***"I have been walking here and there, roaming round the earth"***. We need not imagine what the devil does as he wonders round the earth because the gospel of John 10:10 clarified that the thief (the devil) comes in order to steal, kill and destroy. Thanks, and glory to our Lord and

Saviour Jesus Christ who has come so that we might have life more abundantly. In Christ, we shall continue to be victorious irrespective of the strategies the evil ones have mapped out in order to trap the children of God. Yes, the devil can even cause you to stumble and even fall in some cases; it is not an end in itself. Do not remain where you have fallen; endeavour to rise up and continue with the race because it is not over until it is over. It does not mean too that we should continue falling since God is merciful and will not relent bringing us back to himself whenever we come back. We should not abuse that privilege at all; but always have in mind that we shall reap exactly what we have sown (Galatians 6:7). We should be conscious of the way we live our lives and God will definitely give us the grace to overcome those things that are humanly impossible.

In-so-far-as we live and identify ourselves as Christians, temptations are inevitable but God keeps to his promise; he would not allow us to be tempted beyond our power to remain firm and as at the time we're being put to the test, he promised not only to be with us and strengthen us but would definitely make a way out (1 Cor. 10:13). What matters is the ability to overcome and it is only when we abide in Christ and he abides in us that we can be victorious. I pray that the good Lord will give us the wisdom to know all the devices of the devil as well as the ability to overcome through Christ our Lord; Amen.

CHAPTER 6

JESUS! THE BEST STRATEGY

For every problem in life, there must be solution(s). Life as we all know is full of ups and downs. No matter how difficult or easy the situation may be, **Jesus** is the best strategy to be applied. When the going is good, you need Jesus to direct you on how to effectively utilize your resources to his glory. You need Jesus to guide and guard you in all your doings. You need him to protect you from every hidden danger; you need him to deliver you from the hands of your enemies. You need Jesus to help you in your academic life, in your marital home, in your working places; in fact, in all aspects of your life if at all you want to succeed. We need Jesus in order to be able to overcome the devil and all its antics.

However, in John 8:12, GNT, Jesus says: *"I am the light of the world, whoever follows me will have the light of life and will never walk in darkness".* Also, in John 6:35, Jesus described himself as the bread of life and that those who come to him will never be hungry. He further says that those who believe in him will never be thirsty.

In John 11:25 – 26, GNT, Jesus says: *"I am the resurrection* and life. *Those who believe in me will live, even though they die, and all those who live and believe in me will never die…"* The Lord crowned it all in the following quotations: John 14:6 GNT where he says: *"I am the way, the Truth and the Life; no one goes to the Father except by me."*

In John 15:5 GNT, Jesus says: *"I am the vine and you are the branches. Those who remain in me, and I in them will bear much fruit; for you can do nothing without me".* The last seven words in the above quotation have indeed summarized this chapter because it is only through our Lord and Saviour Jesus Christ that we can succeed in anything we do in life. Remember the saying *"One with Christ is majority".* This was clearly demonstrated in the case between David and Goliath. In I Samuel 17, GNT: David said to Saul, *"Your Majesty, I take care of my father's sheep. Whenever a lion or a bear carries off a lamb, I go after it, attack it and rescue the lamb. And if the lion or beer turns to me, I grab it by the throat and beat it to death. I have killed lions and bears, and I will do the same to this heathen Philistine, who has defied the army of the living God. The Lord has saved me from lions and bears; he will save me from this Philistine".*

David then took his shepherd's stick and then picked up five smooth stones from the stream and put them in his bag with his sling ready, he went out to meet Goliath. The Philistine started walking towards David, with his shield-bearer walking in front of him. He kept coming closer, and when he got a good look at David, he was filled with scorn for him because he was just a nice, good-looking boy. He said to David, *"What is that stick for? Do you think I am a dog? Come on and I will give your body to the birds and animals to eat".* David answered, *"You are coming against me with sword, spear and javelin, but I come against you in the name of the Lord Almighty, the God of the Israelite armies which you have defied. This very day, the Lord will put you in my power; I will defeat you and cut off your head. And I will give the bodies of the Philistine soldiers to the birds and animals to eat. Then the whole world will know that Israel has a God; and everyone else will see that the Lord does not need swords or spears to save his people. He is victorious in battle, and he will put all of you in our power"*.

Goliath started walking towards David again and David ran quickly towards the Philistine's battle line to fight him. He put his hand into his bag and took out a stone, which he slung at Goliath. It hit him in the forehead and broke his skull, and Goliath fell face downwards, David defeated and killed Goliath with a sling and a stone. He ran to him, stood over him, took Goliath's sword out of its sheath, and cut off his head and killed him. When the Philistines saw that their hero is dead, they ran away. David picked up Goliath's head and took it to Jerusalem, but he kept Goliath's weapons in his own tent.

However, there is uncountable number of Goliath of its own kind in the world today, which has been threatening the lives of many. Just as David was able to defeat the then Goliath with the power in the name of the Lord Almighty, you too can be victorious over the Goliath of our time. Our Lord Jesus Christ remains the best strategy in life irrespective of the situation we find ourselves since we can do absolutely nothing without him.

CHAPTER 7

GOD'S PROMISES AND ASSURANCES

The children of God are indeed blessed people to have the word of God at their disposal. Anyone who has the **Word** has *"Everything"* because the word of God is God himself as recorded in the Gospel of John 1:1. The word of God is power; it is victory, healing, blessings, anointing and life itself, etc. In fact, the Holy Scripture contains all we need in life. The issue remains; why do many still suffer without hope, in bondage, not receiving answers to their long-time prayers, living in fear, etc. Many have Bibles of different sizes at home but rarely open any because they have no time for the Word of God. The Lord has so many things in stock for us his children as recorded clearly in Jeremiah 29:11 and in other uncountable portions in the Bible; but we are often short-sighted due to many factors, one of which is lack of time to search through the Scriptures in order to discover what God has in stock for us. Many are actually living in fear and are often threatened to die. This has caused so many people to go to places looking for help where there is absolutely none. Sometimes, their problems are even compounded. Little did such people realize that there is great power in the **Word of God.**

Some of these encouraging passages, promises and assurances of our Lord to us are being outlined below:

- Jeremiah 29:11-12, GNT: *"I alone know the plans I have for you, plans to bring you prosperity and not disaster, plans to bring about the future you hope for. Then, you will call to me. You will come and pray to me, and I will answer you".*

- Jeremiah 30:17, GNT: *"I will make you well again. I will heal your wounds..."*

- Matthew 18:18, GNT: *"What you prohibit on earth will be prohibited in heaven; and what you permit on earth will be permitted in heaven".*

- Mark 16:17 – 18, GNT: *"Believers will be associated with these signs: they will cast out devils in my name, they will speak in strange tongues. If they pick up snakes in their hands, or drink deadly poison, they will not be harmed; they will lay their hands on the sick and they will recover".*

- Luke 10:19, GNT: *"I have given you authority to march on snakes and scorpions and overcome all the power of the enemy and nothing will ever hurt you".*

- Deuteronomy 29:2 – 14, GNT: *"Moses called together all the people of Israel and said to them, "You saw for yourselves what the Lord did to the king of Egypt, to his officials, and to his entire country. You saw the terrible plagues, the miracles, and the great wonders that the Lord performed. But to this very day he has not let you understand what you have experienced. For forty years the Lord led you through the desert, and your clothes and sandals never wore out. You did not have bread to eat or wine or beer to drink, but the Lord provided for your needs in order to teach you that he is your God. And when we came to this place, King Sihon of Heshbon and King Og of Bashan came out to fight against us. But we defeated them, took their land, and divided it among the tribes of Reuben and Gad, and half the tribe of Manasseh. Obey faithfully all the terms of this covenant, so that you will be successful in everything you do. Today you are standing in the presence of the Lord your God, all of you—your leaders and officials, your men, women, and children, and the foreigners who live among you and cut wood and carry water for you. You are here today to enter into this covenant that the Lord your God is making with you and to accept its obligations, so that the Lord may now confirm you as his people and be your God, as he promised you and your ancestors, Abraham, Isaac, and Jacob. You are not the only ones with whom the Lord is making this covenant with its obligations.*

- Isaiah 41:10 – 13, GNT: *"Do not be afraid – I am with you! I am your God - let nothing terrify you! I will make you strong and help you; I will protect you and save you. Those who are angry with you will know the shame of defeat. Those who fight against you will die and will disappear from the earth. I am the Lord your God; I strengthen you and say: do not be afraid, I will help you".*

- John 10:10, GNT: *"The thief comes only in order to steal, kill and destroy. I have come in order that you might have life – in all its fullness"*.

- Isaiah 40:10 – 13, GNT: *"10 The Sovereign Lord is coming to rule with power, bringing with him the people he has rescued. He will take care of his flock like a shepherd; he will gather the lambs together and carry them in his arms; he will gently lead their mothers. Can anyone measure the ocean by handfuls or measure the sky with his hands? Can anyone hold the soil of the earth in a cup or weigh the mountains and hills on scales? Can anyone tell the Lord what to do? Who can teach him or give him advice?*

- John 6:54, GNT: *"Those who eat my flesh and drink my blood have eternal life and I will raise them to life on the last day"*.

- John 6:56, GNT: *"Those who eat my flesh and drink my blood live in me and I live in them"*.

- John 6:35, GNT: *"I am the bread of life, those who come to me will never be hungry; those who believe in me will never be thirsty"*.

- 1 Corinthians 2:9, GNT: *"What no one ever saw or heard, what no one ever thought could happen, is the very thing God prepared for those who love him"*.

- Psalm 46:10, NIV: *"Be still and know that I am God"*.

- Psalm 91:3 – 4, GNT: *"He will keep you safe from all hidden dangers and from all deadly diseases. He will cover you with his wings, you will be safe in his care; his faithfulness will protect and defend you"*.

- Psalm 91:5 – 8, GNT: *"You need not fear any dangers at night or sudden attacks during the day or the plagues that strike in the dark or the evils that kill in daylight. A thousand may fall dead beside you, ten thousand all around you, but you will not be harmed. You will look and see how the wicked are punished"*.

- Psalm 91:9-13 GNT: *"You have made the Lord your defender, the Most High your protector, and so no disaster will strike you, no violence will come near your home. God will put his angels in charge of you, to protect you wherever you go. They will hold you up with their hands to keep you from hurting your feet on the stone. You will trample down lions and snakes, fierce lions and poisonous snakes"*.

- Psalm 91:14 – 16, GNT: *"God says; 'I will save those who love me and I will protect those who acknowledge me as Lord. When they call for me, I will answer them; when they are in trouble, I will be with them. I will rescue them and honour them. I will reward them with long life, I will save them"*.

- Matthew 10:32, GNT: *"For those who declare publicly that they belong to me, I will do the same before my father in heaven"*.

- Matthew 21:22, GNT: *"If you believe, you will receive whatever you ask for in prayer"*.

- John 1:12, NMB: *"To as many as received him, who believe in his name, he gave power to become children of God"*.

- John 15:7, GNT: *"If you remain in me and my words remain in you, then you shall ask for anything you wish, and you shall have it"*.

- Psalm 41:1, GNT: *"Happy are those who help the poor, the Lord will help them"*.

- Exodus 15:26, GNT: *"If you will obey me completely by doing what I consider right and by keeping my commands, I will not punish with any of the diseases I brought to the Egyptians. I am the Lord, the one who heals you"*.

- Matthew 18:2-3 GNT: *So, Jesus called a child to come and stand in front of them, and said, "I assure you that unless you change and become like children, you will never enter the Kingdom of heaven"*.

- Matthew 18:20, NASB: *"Where two or three are gathered in my name, I am there in their midst"*.

- Romans 10:13, KJV: *"Anyone who calls on the name of the Lord shall be saved"*.

- Matthew 5:3, NLT: *"Blessed are the poor in spirit for theirs is the kingdom of heaven"*.

- Isaiah 49:15, GNT: *"Can a mother forget her own baby and not love the child she bore? Even if a mother should forget her child, I will never forget you"*.

- Isaiah 49:16, GNT: *"I can never forget you! I have written your name on the palms of my hands"*.

- Isaiah 49:23, NCV: *"Anyone who puts his trust in me will never be disappointed"*.

- Isaiah 54:10, GNT: *"The mountains and hills may crumble, but my love for you will never end; I will keep for ever my promise of peace"*.

- Zechariah 2:8, GNT: *"Anyone who strikes you, strikes what is most precious to me"*.

- Luke 11:13, GNT: *"Bad as you are, you know how to give good things to your children. How much more, then, will the Father in heaven give the Holy Spirit to those who ask him"*.

- Acts 10:34 – 35, GNT: *"I now realize that it is true that God treats everyone on the same basis. Those who worship him and do what is right are acceptable to him, no matter what race they belong to"*.

- II Thessalonians 3:3, GNT: *"The Lord is faithful, he will strengthen you and protect you from the evil one"*.

- Matthew 18:18, GNT: *"What you prohibit on earth will be prohibited in heaven and what you permit on earth will be permitted in heaven"*.

- II Timothy 1:17, GNT: *"For the Spirit that God has given us does not make us timid; instead, his Spirit fills us with power, love and self-control".*

- Psalm 34:15, GNT: *"The Lord watches over the righteous. He listens to their cries".*

- Psalm 50:15, GNT: *"Call upon me in the time of trouble, I will save you and you will glorify me".*

- Matthew 21:22, GNT: *"If you have faith, you will receive whatever you ask for in prayers".*

- Mark 11:24, GNT: *"When you ask for anything in prayer, believe that you have received it already and it will be yours".*

- James 5:16, GNT: *"The prayer of a good person works powerfully".*

- Isaiah 54:17, GNT: *"No weapon designed against you will succeed."*

- I Corinthians 6:18-20, GNT: *"Avoid immorality. Any other sin a man commits does not affect his body; but the man who is guilty of sexual immorality sins against his own body. Don't you know that your body is the temple of the Holy Spirit, who lives in you and who was given to you by God? You do not belong to yourselves but to God; he bought you for a price. So use your bodies for God's glory."*

- Galatians 6:7, GNT: *"Do not deceive yourselves; God cannot be mocked. A man reaps exactly what he sows"*.

- Matthew 11:28, GNT: *"Come to me all who labour and are overburdened, and I will give you rest"*.

- John 6:35, GNT: *"I am the life-giving bread; anyone who comes to me will never be hungry again; anyone who believes in me will never be thirsty again"*.

- 1Timothy 2:4, GNT: *"God wants all to be saved and to come to the knowledge of the truth"*.

- Isaiah 40:8, GNT: *"The grass withers, the flowers fade, but the word of the Lord remains forever."*

- Matthew 4:4, GNT: *"Man does not live by bread alone, but by every word that comes from the mouth of God"*.

- 1 Corinthians 1:8, GNT: *He will give you the strength to be faithful to the end"*.

- 1 Corinthian 10: 13, GNT: *"Every test that you have experienced is the kind that normally comes to people but God keeps his promise and he will not allow you to be tempted beyond your power to remain firm. At the time you are being put to test, he will give you the strength to endure it and so provide you with a way out.*

- Deuteronomy 20:24, GNT: *"The Lord your God goes with you; he will give you victory"*.

- Psalm 12:6, GNT: *"The promises of the Lord can be trustworthy, they are as genuine as silver, refined seven times in the furnace"*.

- Psalm 118:8, GNT: *"It is better to trust in the Lord than to have confidence in man"*.

- Jeremiah 17:7 – 8, GNT: *"But I will bless those who put their trust in me. They are like trees growing near a stream and sending out roots to the water. They are not afraid when hot weather comes, because their leaves stay green; they have no worries when there is no rain; they keep on bearing fruit."*

- Exodus 14:14, GNT: *"The Lord will fight for you: just keep calm"*.

- Romans 8:31, GNT: *"If God is with us, who can be against us?"*

- Tobit 12:7, GNT: *"Do what is good and no harm will come to you"*.

- Proverbs 18:10, GNT: *"The Lord is a strong tower where the righteous can go and be safe"*.

- Psalm 121:7, GNT: *"The Lord will protect you from all danger; he will keep you safe"*.

- Psalm 128:3, GNT: *"Your wife will be like a fruitful vine in your home, and your children will be like young olive trees round your table"*.

- Isaiah 57:15, GNT: *"I am the high and holy God, who lives for ever. I live in a high and holy place, but I also live with people who are humble and repentant, so that I can restore their confidence and hope."*

- Isaiah 57:18, GNT: *"I have seen how they acted, but I will heal them. I will lead them and help them, and I will comfort those who mourn".*

- Isaiah 60:19, GNT: *"No longer will the sun be your light by day or the moon be your light by night; I, the Lord, will be your eternal light; the light of my glory will shine on you".*

- Isaiah 60:20, GNT: *"Your days of grief will come to an end". I, the Lord, will be your eternal light, More lasting than the sun and moon".*

- Isaiah 60:22, GNT: *"Even your smallest and humblest family will become as great as a powerful nation. When the right time comes, I will make this happen quickly. I am the Lord".*

- Proverb 14:26, GNT: *"Reverence for the Lord gives confidence and security to a man and his family".*

- Deuteronomy 31:6, GNT: *"The Lord your God will be with you; he will neither disappoint nor abandon you".*

- Genesis 12:3, GNT: *"I will bless them that bless you and I will curse them that curse you. And through you I will bless all the nations".*

- 11 Corinthians 5:17, GNT: *"Anyone who is joined to Christ is a new being: the old is gone, the new has come".*

- Exodus 14:14, GNT: *"The Lord will fight for you and there is no need for you to do anything".*

- Exodus 14:13, GNT: *"Don't be afraid! Stand your ground and you will see what the Lord will do to save you today; you will never see these Egyptians again".*

- John 14:1-3, GNT: *"Do not be worried and upset, believe in God and believe also in me. There are many rooms in my father's house, and I am going to prepare a place for you. I would not tell you this if it were not so. And after I go and prepare a place for you, I will come back and take you to myself, so that you will be where I am".*

- Revelation 3:20, GNT: *"Listen! I stand at the door and knock: if anyone hears my voice and opens the door, I will come in and eat with them, and they will eat with me".*

- Isaiah 43:1 – 2, GNT: *"Israel, (insert your name - Millicent) the Lord who created you says, do not be afraid – I will serve you. I have called you by name – you are mine. When you pass through deep waters, I will be with you; your troubles will not overwhelm you. When you pass through fire, you will not be burnt; the hard trials that come will not hurt you".*

- II Chronicles 7:13-14, GNT: *"Whenever I hold back the rain or send locusts to eat up the crops or send an epidemic on my people, if they pray to me and repent and turn away from the evil they have been doing, then I will hear them in heaven, forgive their sins, and make their land prosperous again".*

- Isaiah 43:5, GNT: *"Do not be afraid – I am with you".*

The above are just very few out of the uncountable promises and assurances of God to us – his children. We know actually that God is not man; he keeps to his promises. I can make promises and fail, you can also make promises and not keep to them but our God is infallible, he never fails, not even in his words. Our government have made uncountable number of promises and have failed the masses in diverse ways but our Lord and Saviour Jesus Christ has never and can never fail. Jesus honours his words more than his name (Psalm 138:2). Many are still suffering because they do not know the kind of power at their disposal. There is power; great power in the **Word;** which is God himself. In order not to be denied the abundant blessings, opportunities and privileges of the Lord to us, we need to study the word meticulously and meditatively day-in-day-out. It is the solution to whatever kind of problem in life. Just give it a trial and you shall attest to it.

I pray that the good Lord will help you to discover the great power in his **Word.** May this word be planted in your heart just like the seed planted by the riverside, that bears great fruits in season and out of season, in the Mighty name of Jesus, Amen.

CONCLUSION

There is absolutely nothing that should separate us from the love of God. The love of God for us is incomparable; that is why Christ came to the world and died a shameful death on the Cross; even while we were still sinners. God has the best of all plans for us in life as recorded in Jeremiah 29:11, ESV. He is indeed beckoning on us to lean on him and live. He says: ***"Behold I stand at the doors of your hearts knocking, anyone who hears my voice and open, I will enter"*** (Revelation 3:20 KJV). Let us therefore open our hearts for the Lord to come in and dwell since we can do absolutely nothing without him. Every other thing in life has the possibility of failing anyone, anytime, anywhere, but Christ has never and can never fail. You will not be an exception if you lean on him sincerely.

However, do not let your heart be troubled because of the difficult moment you are facing in life for Christ is able to deliver you from all, he will turn your tears to cheers and as well restore your lost hope in no small measure. Everything in life has expiry dates including your worries and every challenge that comes your way. They will surely expire by the special grace of God. All you need do is to lean on Christ faithfully with your whole heart; you will discover that the Lord is indeed good.

MEMORARE

*R*emember, *O most gracious Virgin Mary, that never was it known that anyone who fled to thy protection, implored thy help, or sought thine intercession was left unaided. Inspired by this confidence, I fly unto thee, O Virgin of virgins, my mother; to thee do I come, before thee I stand, sinful and sorrowful. O Mother of the Word Incarnate, despise not our petitions, but in thy mercy hear and answer us, Amen.*

Printed in the United States
By Bookmasters